The Wrack Line

~

Pat Hanahoe-Dosch

FUTURECYCLE PRESS
www.futurecycle.org

Library of Congress Control Number: 2017941032

Copyright © 2017 Pat Hanahoe-Dosch
All Rights Reserved

Published by FutureCycle Press
Athens, Georgia, USA

ISBN 978-1-942371-31-1

For my brother, David J. Dosch,
2/5/66–4/29/16

Contents

IV.

I.

Where You Have Gone

We wandered through the Khan-el-Kalili bazaar,
surrounded by baskets of turmeric, cumin, coriander, cinnamon,
bins of linden, rosehip, sage and black teas,
buying samples of everything.

You left before we visited the pyramids. I became a tourist alone.
Gravel trickled down from the space where the Sphinx's nose used to breathe.

On my bedroom shelf, the Egyptian glass bottles you gave me still
perfume my room with a scent of rose petals. I keep them
empty, glass stoppers loosely set in their throats.

Tonight an Egyptian boy, maybe sixteen, sits at the cafe table
where we last ate together, sipping mint tea
in the uncertain evening light. He is stroking an oud. His music

is the sounds of traffic around Tahrir Square, light
dimming in the hallways in the museum of antiquities,
the darkness encased inside a sarcophagus.

You have become a grain of sand rolling across the Sinai Desert
in the mouth of a hot, African wind.

You are a small rock a tourist tosses
from the rest area at the top of Mount Sinai,
the trash-littered cement and gravel square lined
with stone seats that look out upon the sunrise like stone tablets,
commandments, commitments aching to be broken.

You are the grit in a ridge below St. Catherine's monastery.
You are the dried out, prickly remains of the burning bush.

You are broken bits of gravel embedded in the rubber sole of a monk's shoe,
dust and sand layered into the leather of a Bedouin's sandal,
the crust on the underside of a camel's hoof.

How to Deal with an Ex

You are not dead.
But I am laying you out, not embalmed,
but empty of all blood and movement,
stretched flat for viewing in biodegradable wood,
dressed in last weekend's suit and tie.
What we did. What we didn't.
Let your arms rest just so, crossed
over your chest, the one I lay my head on
to listen to your heart as it slowed its rapid beating.
I am not burying you, but
cremating your memories in such a conflagration
I will never be able to look at you again, no matter what temptation,
not even a sealed space, full of nothing.
I will say no prayer, no eulogy.
Eventually even this memory will distill before the wind,
a swirl of dust and ash across a river's surface.
When I see you in the street, you will be
just another ghost passing through,
looking for a medium who doesn't exist.

Salutations

from the levees of New Orleans, then onward
to the Red River waters to cleanse the volcanic disturbances

of our canceled wedding reception from which
I have absconded. Tell the priest the Nature Conservancy

would like the arches of his cathedral returned soon.
The stone angels will not be mistaken for the natural transformations

of normal lava flow. Hawaii is next.
Without you it may be just ethnography. And yet.

Fare well and so forth. There are vineyards in Napa I want to see.
Maybe someday I'll journey back

to NJ. Probably not to you. Please forgive me.
There are moments when I miss you.

To the Lover Who Lied About Being Divorced

And then you disappeared.
You missed these years I had to choose
between color and curls
because my thin hair can't hold both.
I chose to hide the gray, to leave behind
those brunette half-moons and ringlets,
a style for which I paid so dearly in my thirties,
a temporary decade, like me, one you left behind
with no regrets, no investment, nothing to mark
you were ever a part of it. I have photos
of myself, permed hair rounding up
my sharp nose and small mouth. None of you.
I tossed them into the recycling bin.

I accept the mass of straight, blonde lines
my hair has become, lines like a spider might ride
from web to ground, one home to another.
My mouth is a tighter, horizontal line now.
The creases around the edges
of my lips and eyes are sliced more clearly,
but these are the healed cuts,
scarred boundaries laid bare, lines
you crossed over and over.

What you won't see: the roots grow back, gray.
Always they grow back, no matter how
much peroxide burns along my scalp.
And the permanent cut I still hold
is scissored open again every time the damaged ends
are trimmed away to keep the shape,
dyed and disguised, far away from the natural curls
across the waning moon of your wife's face.

Through a Glass, Bitterly

It is always the dark past in the mirror:
my mother, her mother, her sister, their aunts
collect around my image. They wave,
frown, glare. They walk
into the room, as though really there.
I hear them whisper:
what did you do to your hair?
Wear a bra and stand up straight.
Who is he? Who are you, really?
Their grim Catholic prayers
are shards of glass in my dreams. Their stories
have annealed mine.
I no longer know who I am
staring at through the looking glass. We are
always at the mercy of our ghosts.
Even the cellulite on my thighs
reminds me of my mother, her legs,
the way she hid from cameras in middle age.
The voice I speak with has become
the echo of my mother, her mother,
and so on. There is no exorcism
strong enough to banish these women.
They grow stronger with each year.
I did not know them all, and yet
I have this aunt's eyes, that great-aunt's nose,
this one's height, that one's ears,
my grandmother's mouth, her arthritic bones,
my mother's temper, her anger,
the uncertainties, questions, betrayals,
the doubts and fears, large and small.
They gather in our glass cage.
There is no old age
bearable enough to live with them all.

Inheritance

For all the aging women I know

If instead of a camel
when you glare into a mirror,
you saw the swirl of light the moon refracts
when you eye it through a telescope,

perhaps the teeth of the camel
would not bite quite so sharply,
drawing bits of blood when you swallow
the kisses your child left on the kitchen counter.

Perhaps the gray chin hairs you pluck
with tweezers twice a week
might not feel like a desert rat's whiskers or tail
if you could see in the mirror
what your daughter sees
or searches for: a hint, a map

for how she will sally through her own nights,
her own passage by the light of the moon
or other satellite of her own choosing,
her own eyes choosing or not

to welcome desert creatures or other sad myths
into the spaces between the kisses she owns
and the mirrors she will one day wear
like contacts, lenses to sharpen or alter
what other visions she aspires to.

You are the telescope she peers through now,
your light, the gift of glass focused on the bits of suns
breaking into galaxies through the black universe.

Nothing

(After Gregory Orr)

What did you mean? he asks.
Nothing, she says. It was nothing,
like the nothing of your absence
for days, no phone call, no email,
the nothing of your silences,
like the nothing of the furnace
that won't turn on and leaves the house
cold in January in the first
serious frost of the night,
or the way empty chairs slump
around an empty kitchen table
while the microwave blinks
that nothing is finished
cooking and ready to eat.
This is the nothing of Sunday mornings,
quietly turning in bed to find
nothing there, the empty space
like the nothing left behind
in an empty house, for sale,
furniture and belongings all removed,
papers signed and delivered,
only dust left to settle anywhere
or nowhere, the nothing of doors
opening into rooms where no one
lives anymore, the nothing of nights
when nothing at all happens, nothing
but the occasional cockroach or mouse
searching through nothing left behind,
and somewhere, she is nowhere
to be found, nothing left
of the nothing they both finished
leaving for no one, their absence, their silences.

Why They Sold the House

Here are the chips and cracks of what was spoken,
or was not. There is the quiet of her anger,
here, the hyperbolic breath, the inhalation of his carefully structured
indifference, and there, the cruelty of closed glass doors,
shut against the flowering dogwood and azaleas,
the backyard's lush exhalation, oxygen puddles of sunlight
sparkling with static from the windows, the shutters, the aluminum
siding and other bits of the house that have ingested
the bitterness, glistening like an oil spill of his resentments,
her frustrations, and all the pinched words they finally let go,
and here is the way the house listens:
the water in the basement, the clogged toilets,
the leaking furnace, like blood
slowly leaking from a deep cut, or brush burns seared across
arms and legs, or the purification of a leech placed near a vein,
a medieval will to balance the humors.

Talking to My Dead Sister
on the Anniversary of Her Death

> "Break the glass   shout
> and break the glass   force the room"

—Jean Valentine

I am sitting at the kitchen table,
drinking green tea and listening
to the very loud clock in the next room nag:
I must leave soon. Morning
light is only beginning to brighten
the corners of each window.
In these long years without you I've learned
you really won't ever talk to me again,
or write a letter, or call, or be here, or
forgive me a multitude of small cruelties.
Your children are grown, married, have
children, houses, jobs. I think they're happy,
though your absence gouged a detour
they haven't quite GPS'd their way out of yet.
I'd like to know if you are only
those bones cluttering the casket in your grave,
or if some part of you is somewhere,
exasperated at our longing, trying to

shatter the glass and leap   into the air's momentum,
    lighting up trees and air   sparks from a campfire
  someone threw a thick branch into   leaving no burn,
no ash, no smoke, to scatter   ecstatically in the air,
    flashing through the long night   so many of us sleep through.

It's time for me to leave,
and you're still not talking.

Thanksgiving Dinner

We talk and talk; we sit and pass around
more wine, potatoes, turkey, yams and peas.
We cannot hear each voice for all the sound.

Outside, the cold blows trash across the ground.
The kitchen's heat seeps into the room as we drink tea.
We talk and talk, we sit and pass around

pies and more wine and tea. We are bound
by manners and grit to ignore history.
We cannot hear each voice for all the sound.

The children run, screeching, jumping, all wound
up with sugar and toys. They don't understand the key
is to talk and talk, to sit and pass around

the stories and jokes that say little, but go round
past betrayals, tensions, differences; please,
we cannot hear each voice for all the sound.

This is the one time of year we are all bound
to gather in one place though no one sees
how we talk and talk, sit and pass our lives around.
We cannot hear each voice for all the sound.

II.

How to Catch a Monarch

Smear your hands with pollen
and stand still like a tree
rooted into the lawn by a flowering
bush of purple blossoms like firecrackers
and hold your hands, palms out,
motionless, pollen stains skyward.
If you stand long enough,
like a sycamore in your backyard,
like milkweed hushed in doldrums before sunset,
one might land and settle softly
on your arced, stiff fingers, wanting the pollen,
but gracing you with a ripple
of an earthquake two continents away,
like all things of air and blossom
that wander into your embrace.

Honestly, Really, Truly, Actually Stop Using the Word 'Literally'

Literally nothing has happened in my life since last week, he said.
Figuratively, though, I said, surely the air flowed around you
in waves, perhaps even stirring a typhoon across Japan, and your hands
glowed like fish wallowing in the shallow waters near
the Fukushima nuclear power plant, or at least moved to feed your mouth
like a backhoe slowly re-filling a grave after a funeral.

Surely your eyes saw something,
like sonar fanning the ocean currents for anomalies on the sea floor;
your ears must have listened to your teachers and the world around you
the way NOAA's buoy sensors listen to data, track a tsunami wave
hurtling from one continent to another, shouting the news by satellite
to warning systems in the path of death by water.

He stared at me as though I were a tsunami alarm blaring unexpectedly:
fishermen might leap into their boats, catch left rotting on the wharfs,
desperate to ride past the wave before it hits the shore, to wait out
the crash of water, a demon of destruction from the depths of—
No, he said, I literally did not do any of that.
He fled as though a giant wave were cresting and falling behind him,
as though a tsunami couldn't catch him and drown
all the literal moments of his day in brine and radioactive sea water.

Taps

1.

Every night he falls into sleep
    to "Taps" played over loudspeakers
        on wooden poles. Every night, the sound
of a trumpet or bugle playing that song.
    Every night, in the space
        between awake and dying
dream: his sister's coffin perched above its grave,
    waiting to be lowered into it,
        green felt draping the edges,
white carnations scattered along the lid like rain.
    Stabbed to death by her ex-husband.

2.

Every night, he unfurls
    into his sleeping bag, into
        the same song the Army plays
every night
    and at funerals.
        Then he wakes into an Afghan morning, silent and dark.
The base wakes every morning
    to sand brushing against tent walls,
        to the heat, like a crematorium.

3.

Except some days they are missing someone. Or another.
    Some days tap along in the dust,
        some days don't. Some days

are for explosions and shrapnel and bits of shredded skin.
    Some days tap into night with just enough
        rain so poppies can grow, red stains
blossoming
    in rivulets across mountains
        where women are masked in blue drapes
or buried in mud walls.

Malala

What is a symbol or a hero, but a human
story told over and over, a photo,
a name, a recounting, a bullet in the head,
blood smeared across the wooden seats of a van?

She gives her story to us
for the others, left behind among the veiled
and scarved lives in a space walled in by some
of the most beautiful mountains in the world.

Their treacherous, jagged peaks sharpen against the sky
while the snows swirl and avalanche
across their faces, scoring crevasses and dark scars
across the rock of their bodies like acid
thrown across the skin of girls

who want to learn enough to glimpse
what might lie beyond
those impassable borders. Mud brick and stone walls,
a few rugs, blankets and bitter winds
separate their villages from ours,
a deeper and colder rift
than the expanse between our continents.

Malala's Mother, the First Week

In what empty ravine of rocks and dirt
does her hungry mind drift now that we
can feed only her body, which we sting with fluids and medicine?
Once I starved to know more, too,
than how to cook dahl or pray for a calm house.
I could see winds whirl the snows on the sharp, jagged
mountains that surround us. I wanted
to know what stirred those icy flakes and currents,
yet kept them there on those steep peaks
they cannot escape
unless the wind blows them far enough down
where they can melt in the sun, come summer and release.
I wanted to know how to read the Koran myself and not
depend on these sharp, jagged men
to tell me what it says I should be. I want
so much more for my daughter than I could ever swirl into
in this life. *Here is how you find*
the area of a triangle, my husband, a teacher, once explained.
To know the depth of these mountains, to be able to calculate
the distance between them—that is the greatest gift
any of us can give her. She can read
the Koran. She knows
it does not forbid her an education.
These men are angry and afraid because they cannot tell her
what they want her to believe. She can
calculate the area between their sharp corners and betrayals.
She can be so much more than these mountains
frame. If only she can heal enough now. If only
they have not caused such an avalanche
in her brain that she cannot climb back to me.
I listen to the sound of her labored breathing and I know
she is scaling the ridges and crevasses they have made.
I know she is gripping the rocks and ledges of her memory
and climbing slowly back to me, one handhold and foothold at a time.

Arab Spring

Now the god Set prowls the Cairo streets
in a Mercedes Benz in starlight,
blocking lanes of trucks, vans, busses,
because he can. Because the night
is always his mansion.

Salah ad-Din's shadow sips the black emptiness
in Bir Yusef, the well, what little is left
of the original Citadel he built to rule Egypt:
his black visage visits on nights when the crescent
moon is a tipped over candle dripping just enough
to light the minarets and dome of the mosque

on the great fortress, whose stones whisper
to the gods of ancient ghosts who still wander,
too poor for the rites of the dead.
Even now, Salah ad-Din raises his sword to the crusaders,
but no one in Tahrir Square can see him: there is too much

light, anger, and fire.
The Nile is a black, glistening cobra.
Set sings to her. She rises, hissing under the bridges,
her throat widening, fangs aimed at the roads slithering beside her.
But even the Nile cannot douse the burning city.

The dead watch.
Tourists walk through them in the daylight.
Someone builds a bomb. A soldier cocks his pistol.
The roads are a snarl of ash, dirt, metal and rubber
bleating. It's not too late.

There's still hope in the crowds,
chanting across the city. American journalists

still write about spring and new beginnings
in this jaded city, where the poor
haunt the dead, living in tombs or huts by graves in Al-erafa:
a woman cooks curry in a stove two feet
from a marble, inlaid grave, near her bed in the mausoleum.

It's winter. The night is not unbearably hot yet:
stars glitter on the windshield as Set drives
toward Giza and what is left
of an ancient world he cannot leave too far
behind in his rearview mirror.

Why Did the Tourist Cross the Road?

"When the moment comes, take the last one
from the left."
—Chinese fortune cookie

It's monsoon season and
the Yamuna River has swamped
rice paddies, farms,
concrete and glass buildings, turnpikes
and dirt roads in Delhi.

Huts of mud, thatch, wood, plastic tarps,
blue and green spots in the brown, muddy waters
dot the crests of trees, tiers of mud and green rice plants
like orderly, tall grasses peering in patches
from the water rippling and writhing around itself.

Families watch traffic from tents of patched canvas tarps
stretched over round, wooden poles, lined up
along the dirt and gravel by the side of the highway.

No one notices
me weaving from one corner towards the other.
Families cook on roofs, laundry draped over walls, porches, steps.

A light brown cow with ears perched upright
saunters down the middle of the road.
Cars, trucks, auto rickshaws swerve around it,
honking to let the animal know they are coming
up on the left or right. It keeps walking.

I will see it still walking hours later
as I stare from the hotel window,
though by then it might be a different cow
with the same attitude.

Now I am standing still, a rock in the middle
of this turbulent current. If I step a little closer
to where even the motor bikes cannot swerve,

what ancient god will spare me? Is there
a protector of street crossings? A god
armed with a whistle and stop sign,
a god of the traffic light disregarded?

Three hundred and thirty million Hindu gods.
Is there one
who will bless macadam and tar,
stop the farce of road rules?
Right now, there is only the holy Yamuna,
who will dry up in a month or two.

The hotel waits. The air-conditioned room,
western toilet, bottles of safe water, TV and soft pillows
wait. Another cow crosses, unchallenged,

safe and unremarkable
as it searches for edible grass and weeds
growing along the dirt and trash of the borders
between highway and fields, city and tourists, refugees,
villagers cooking over small wood fires in one hundred degrees
by the side of the road next to their disaster relief
tents, as everyone waits

for flood waters to recede
as the large city drives on around them,
honking and shedding exhaust
though they do not join this modern dance of Shiva.

I take the last steps to the left of a bus to the other side,

through the security check point,
my air conditioned room, and
cable TV, flashing videos
of floodwaters receding through a marble temple,
leaving behind mud, a shoe, fragments
of statues: a hand, a leg poised to dance on its toes. And
a small wooden Buddha, a ceramic cow:
Kamadhenu, a goddess floating among sewage and holy water.

Why the Wind Makes That Sound

It was the relief of the gray and brown albatross
faltering in its descent
in one moment in a gust of wind,
then folding its wings and walking tipsily
across the sand speckled with footprints of other gulls.

It was the relief of the small dog shark
finally swimming all the way through a riptide
that had pulled it into the waves and shallow water,
finally passing the sandbar and breaking away
from that irresistible, implacable pull.

It was the relief of the wild horse rolling in the sand,
rubbing its back across the coarse grains
to douse the burn and itch of summer,
mosquito and fly bites, trickles of blood
dribbling along its flanks and legs,
washed by the salt water it runs through after rising.

It was the relief of the girl,
lying back in the hot sand, towel
bunched under her head,
sunlight braising her sore feet, her long legs
stretched toward the tide line, her whole, young body
cocooned in sand and salt air, which she thinks
will never ask anything of her, even as the tide
laps stealthily toward her.

It was the relief of the waves finally broken
and stretched before the wrack line
before sliding back into the green,
black, blue, liquid universe.

Flight

Here are the feathers
to offer the wind, to mend
the rifts in the currents
your passing through will spread.

There are the cedars,
from your height, like green feathers,
swaying and rippling along
the rivers and ridges of the land's skin
to guide you, your map
over a surface of fractures and scars.

Here is rain to weigh
you down again, to soak your fine pores
and breath, to bring you close again
to loam and mulch, knobby branch and crusty bark.

There is the cairn, a marker of stones
to clasp your tired limbs, your folding wings,
the moment you settle for the end, the weight
of gravity tethering you at last.

Here is the wind to lift you up again.
There is the tree whose leaves will wave you on.
These are all harbingers of grief,
shadows trees cast over stones.

Surrender

The black teenager raised his arms,
palms wide and flat against the air.
Roses bloomed from his chest anyway,
petals dripping on the asphalt.
A warm night breeze carried some
of the petals in its breath, scattered them
across stoops and alleyways. Some
were crushed between people's feet. Some
tapped on windows. Some knocked on doors. Some
rolled into street gutters and wept. Some
were picked up and carried in the palms of children. Those
grew into roses and multiplied. Women, children,
teens and men dropped rose petals on streets and lawns
when they knelt and opened their palms wide into the air.
More petals swirled across asphalt in a growing wind.
More petals cloyed the air but were overcome
by tear gas, bullets, the stench
of gasoline and gunpowder.
It was a summer of wild thorns and perfume.
Roses grew in cracks in asphalt and concrete.
Some leaned against the boy's gravestone.
Most rotted into compost.
Some of the roses became blood and water.
Some became skin and anger.
Some became pollen on the hind legs of bees.

Surrender 2

The black teenager raises his arms in surrender, palms flat against the air.
He knows the cops will shoot, otherwise. He raises no gun, no knife,
no fists. But a cop is frightened, anyway, and shoots. A whole city smokes
in anger and fear. The cop is even more afraid, after.

The teens on the streets are afraid. But they swear and carry signs
with bravura. The women in the grocery stores are afraid. But they carefully
choose the ripest tomatoes, cheapest bread. Men walking, driving cars,
sitting in a bus, are afraid. But some sip beer, or gin, or iced tea, or bottles
of water. Men and women watch out windows, stand in doors, walk
home, afraid. Some make spaghetti sauce or salad, barbeque hot dogs
or hamburgers. They go to work; they look for work. Or not.
Children go to school. At night, they all walk and carry signs with bravura.

Somewhere there are people watching the news unafraid, saying, *This is not
my America. Those are not my streets.* Sirens flash by. They go to other streets.
There are borders there, lines drawn where a street cannot be white,
a fence cannot be black.

Women are walking in the streets, men, teens, children between them.
The borders are lined blue and red. Nobody crosses police lines. Nobody
crosses the crowds' lines. Crossroads and guns. People on this side of the
border hide their guns. People on the other side wave guns in the air.
This is not South Africa. This is not back-in-the-day.

Let's do a remake, a metamorphosis, a revolution: here
is a peach, a plum, a donut. These are our hands. We are carrying
only food. Here, take an apple, a glass of water, or wine. Here is a slice
of cake, or pie, or bread. Here are our hands. They are empty, palms wide
against the air, waiting for your touch.

Ode to a Rug

Red wool: colors of the Sonoran sun
setting across red sandstone. Green
wool at the edges: green of desert grass,
weeds growing in clumps between rocks.
Red of the desert: Arizona, Utah. Mojave
shadows scratching across a butte or ridge
cracked by fault lines, geometric shapes
cut into red rocks. Mesquite and jojoba,
tiny green along the trails circling
deepening shades of red. No birds.
No mallet chiseling human meaning.
Just Navajo dyes on wool. The gift
of warp and weft, a woman's voice
still singing patterns in the fibers.

This Oven-Vault of a City

1.

In the dark of my small orange tent,
I am faceless.
A man in a trailer
in the campsite next to mine hums
as he removes his clothes under the dim lightbulb
inside. He is shadow gesturing oddly in the windows.
Then he is all darkness.
There is no relief even in the night
from the suffocating heat
and humidity as I lie
on an air mattress in a campground
on the edge
of a levee of New Orleans

2.

where I wandered all day—
faceless, voiceless, just another
ghost haunting this hurricane of history
in one of the cities of the dead—
gawking at its oven-vault tombs,
a tourist riding a bus, shooting a photo,
walking through the famous cemeteries,
then the ninth ward of houses
still vacant or destroyed from Katrina, marks of body counts
still sprayed across a few of their faces, and then
back to the French Quarter, the oldest houses,
standing on a corner where there are no signs
to say this was once the spot
where slaves were auctioned.

Now it's a simple street corner
with a hotel on one side, Spanish and French
balconied houses crumbling along the street
all around it. Cars stop and go.
Tourists wander, faceless in this heat,
without seeing
the black shadows flailing from the past
as streetlamps take over
in the quickening night.

3.

Downtown, in the French Quarter,
the parties and drinking,
music, laughing, and all other sorrows,
are just beginning. In the gaslight and shadows,
white and black colors sharpen in contrast.
Everyone is faceless. All the voices,
even the shadows', blend
in the loud cacophony of night.

Nada

She sets the cups of coffee
on a table by rolls of flatware and paper napkins.
White, thick plastic mugs filled
with what looks like cedar water with a slight
sheen of oil glazing the surface.
The women don't look at her.
The men just glance quickly to see
if she's pretty. They don't look
at her eyes. She writes their wishes
on a small square of paper
and clips it to the window
of the kitchen where the cook
will grant their requests
with more grease and salt than they expect.

This is not a clean, well-lighted place.
She imagines them driving away
to a mile-long, three-story brick house
with a fountain in the front yard—say a ceramic one
with frogs around the bowl, spouting clear water—
and maybe leaving enough
of a tip so she could get a bus ticket
and spend a week on a beach in Florida.
The snow here is black with dirt
and packed into piles of ice that won't melt
until late March. The beauty
of snow on the covers of Christmas cards
has long been buried under the carbon of car exhaust,
factory exhalations, and mud from tires.

It's January and already winter
has become a cliché from a bad novel.
This diner only offers
heat from the kitchen and the manager's

bad temper. It's warm enough,
but not enough to break the curse of gray sleet,
slippery walks, roads and gutters
sputtering with snow melt. But
the tip is not enough even for
a glass of sangria after work
in the bar across the street. She will have to settle
for the beer one of the other regulars
will buy her, again, as he does, every night,
even though she never does more than say, *Thanks*.

Driving Through Kansas

Yellow-tasseled corn the color of grasshoppers
and wheat the color of the dust and dirt
between road and field, ripple
the width and length of the Kansas plains on all sides
of the black strip of freeway within the bowl-shaped
horizons encircling all like distant
blue-and-white stained fences. The only relief
comes from fleeting clumps of black and white, or brown, cows
and occasional puffs of sheep. If a tree
rustles and bows, graciously, in the breath
the day's heat exhales continuously, it is a momentary
glimpse of vertical life, shadows hovering protectively around
a farmhouse, barn, or silo. Such sightings are islands
of bark, leaves, wood streaked with white paint, iron or tin
colors, sparks of sunlight off glass windows, in a wide sea
of yellowing grass pastures streaked
with piles of cow dung and cracked earth, torn up
by hooves, heat, or darker weather churning across the plains.

As the day grows, so does the wind; by evening,
even billboards flutter and knock
against the air as though trying to escape the plains.
The bowl of horizons now revolves in slow circles, moving
as black clouds slowly accumulate like mud in a pigsty,
and rain, when it comes, falls from the black aerial accumulation
like spit, then harder; then the thunder and wind,
stomping and groaning like a herd of cows,
and then the lightning, fire-lit veins along the planet's outer skin
and, finally, hail, discarded teeth
thrown onto the thirsty ground, which, greedy and fecund,
slowly absorbs it all.

In the morning, outside my hotel, only the battered face
of a handicap sign remains
as evidence of what has passed. It lies
an inch from my van's tires. The windshield is unbroken
and washed clean, like everything else
in the parking lot and fields surrounding the truck stop,
a gas, oil, and junk food haven beside the asphalt that divides
field from field, from another field, and another,
and the Biblical billboards, the exits that beg all passing through to love
a god of hail, thunder, and flood.

Driving through Utah

Cracks and wrinkles in blue skin
sliver across the desert sky
like streaks of clouds.
The left and right horizons
are fractured jaw lines and coffee-stained teeth.
The desert seems flat,
but beyond the asphalt
lumps of sand spotted with tufts of grass
rise and fall: the moles and pores
of Utah's skin. Then a butte
and ridges, a wall
like shards of dark glass slicing into a brown back
bent forward at the waist from hard labor.

The acrid air abrades even human skin.
Funnels of wind
rise and dissipate
in the distance: rust red,
burnt orange sand and gravel. The turn
to Moab and the National Park
promises fossilized dunes, like layers of stretch marks
and cellulite across the belly,
and geologic fractures,
beauty framing the blue, leaking sky
and tears of sunlight
between round windows and arches
of granite and sandstone,

formations like abstract sculptures and sand paintings,
earth's narratives told through wind and fractures.
Tourists' car radios, cameras,
caravans of RVs and plastic water bottles
flood humans into this space,

a hot wind billowing out of the horizon,
a haze that distorts the landscape
into photos and family vacations.

We are all guilty of mixing metaphors
and waxing anthropomorphic as tourists
here. The arches continue to stretch and lean
despite the people hiking and posing around them.
Snakes, lizards and scorpions, ravens,
rabbits, yucca, pinion pines, prickly pear cactus
grow anyway. The sands burn and cool, shift
and erode, despite the asphalt road
that circles back to the entrance of the park.
The desert and mountains
stretch and streak and wind and drop and rise before us
because that's how we see them. In the end,
we are just living bones flailing before we join them.

Wrong Turn in PA

The guy in the big, green Chevy Malibu
cuts me off as I swerve into the turn lane,
passes, barely missing my front bumper.
I honk, because I'm from NJ and that's
what we do there, and then
I follow him in the turn lane, blinker on,
but he stops. Just parks his car
in the left turn lane, gets out,
walks toward me, shouting, *What's your problem, bitch?*

I roll down my window. It's ten degrees out
but I shout he cut me off,
I'm trying to turn left,
and if he doesn't move, I'm calling the cops.
Better yet, I say, *maybe I'll just
shove your car out of the way with my
front bumper.* I can't help it.
I'm from Jersey. He's cursing,
threatening me as he stands in the road
and I tell him, *Really? All it would take is my foot
to go just a little deeper on the pedal here...*

Another car drives past and honks.
The man turns around, screams at the car
that has driven on, then turns back
and keeps yelling. I can't hear what he's saying.
He's just some character escaped
from a Tarentino movie
trying to figure out what happened that landed him
here in an empty road screaming empty sounds
like a toddler locked in a room.
I drive around him,
yelling out the window, *Get a therapist!*
and he jumps back, perhaps thinking I am really
going to hit him with my car.

I'm from New Jersey. I believe
compassion and driving
don't mix. But I can't resist.
I feel sorry enough for him
that I leave him standing in the turn lane,
no cops, no one to scream at, only
the turn he rushed to take ten minutes ago,
still there, still untaken.

Lancaster

"The feeling that a particular place is suffused with memories, the specific focus of sacred and profane stories, and that the whole landscape is a congeries of such places, is what is meant by a local sense of the land."

—Barry Lopez, *Arctic Dreams*

1.

Tobacco leaves hang from barn rafters
like long, stringy bats dangling from plain wood beams.

A pair of horses trudge along the dirt road
dragging a cart between multitudes
of green corn ears dripping silk strings,
stalks so high, the man driving the horses can't see
over the tassels shivering in the breeze.

Five brown and white cows by a wire fence
stand in mud and manure, twitch an ear, a tail.
Water in a cement trough glistens in the sunlight.

No telephone poles or wires frame the wooden house
at the edge of the fields. Clotheslines
crisscross the grass and dirt yard.
Gray, black and blue dresses, shirts and pants
flap before whitewashed walls
like bruises in the air.

A square plastic crate cages a calf.
Someone's veal-to-be. Broiled.
The calf lies there, eyes opening and closing.

Nearby, fresh tobacco grows in a narrow field,
leaves clumped together, wide,
stilled fan blades resting in the black, crumbling dirt.

A clapboard sign points tourists and locals
down the dirt road through the corn:
Fresh eggs. Homemade butter and pies.
I drive down the dirt
to buy a dozen eggs and a roll of Amish butter.

2.

A woman saunters across the street,
says: *Yeah, sure, shine that*
floodlight right in her eyes so she can't see.
Nice going, pretending
she's talking to the woman walking next to her
and not the cop who pulled me over.
They cross the street and go around
the two police cars and my pulled-over Prius.
I ain't afraid of no cops, says the other,
but that's all I hear.
They disappear down a side street.

The city cop gives me a ticket. In the rear-view
mirror I see another
on the corner with a rifle,
standing guard, as though this
downtown section of Lancaster City
is dangerous. No one else
walks by or opens a window.

Cars drive by. Ten blocks
away art galleries and restaurants
flash and sparkle with people, decorative
lights, the noise of crowds
and open windows entertaining
wanderers with money. Ten miles away
there are farms, a black horizon

of fields, fences, barns, house windows
lit by kerosene lanterns.

A man opens his door, sits on the cracked,
flaking concrete step
of his front stoop, watching.
He rolls a cigarette, lights it, blows smoke
toward the cops as though to prove
it's just tobacco.
A baseball cap hides his face.
He raises his middle finger to us all.

3.

Crows are rarely silent.
Some mornings, though,
they just watch
from the bunker of a tree in full leaf
as I walk past. Today
as I hike around the cemetery lot, the only
level landscape
in this neighborhood where I live along Bean Hill,
the chieftain of the flock—
as tall as a small headstone,
wings as wide as the width
of the graves I pass—
this chief of crows just watches
till I pass,
headed toward a copse of pines
sheltering Our Lady of Sorrows
circle, separate from the Cross of Christ
rectangular crop of more expensive graves.

He rises,
this oil-slick colored, feathered, alpha crow,
flies in a widening circle above me,
calling to the others in those pines

who answer, then rise,
fly off in a scattered mass,
perch in trees at the other end of the cemetery,
protesting my presence,
settling among the pine needles
to watch as I trespass.

I pass an old woman
by a grave. She places a bouquet
of lilies next to a headstone
as I try not to look
at the grief in her bowed back.
A beige pickup waits for her
by the side of the road. The driver
tosses a cigarette butt out the window.
It smolders briefly on the asphalt.
I can hear my feet crunch tiny stones and dirt
as I turn down an unpaved side road,
past a granite St. Francis of Assisi,
toward my house, which is still,
after ten years, not quite home.

III.

What the Tide Brings:

Surf clams, quahogs, horse mussels, bay scallops,
channeled whelks, skate egg casings,
green and black strands of rockweed and kelp.

A laughing gull and a least tern waddle and skip
along the wrack line, stop to feast on a small skate,
washed up dead. A great black-backed gull circles above,
drops a clam onto the damp sand to break the shells
and expose the flesh.

A northern moon snail shell, empty between a cluster
of seaweed and a dead spider crab.

Alive, the snail can hug a clam with its one large foot,
then lick a hole through the shell and suck the meat
into its mouth. One of my parents' neighbors
eats those snails, clams, mussels, scallops, whelks, crabs,
any succulent flesh encased in a shell
he can scavenge, fish, or trap.

The tide's detritus, its cast-offs, the wrack line.

What the water and sand can't hide, bury, or shape,
some creature will eat. What is left, the ocean
swallows, later: my footprints, yours,
sea-glass, shell fragments, bones and last wishes.
Wrack and ruin. Digestion,
the waves' great purpose.

You and I, digging a hole, searching for sand crabs.

We are attacked by sand fleas and green head flies.
For some reason, you laugh
when I slap at the insects.
For no reason, I swear
the ocean's appetite is another kind of laughter.

Preterition

The hurricane dissipates:
    the fragile line between
    insult and rage, grief and loss,
    this wrack line
    the surf leaves behind
litters driveways, sidewalks, asphalt,
sand piled like snow across streets and lawns.

The surf still laps at shop windows:
once again a softer crash
and swallow along the coastline.

The island has shut down.
Almost everyone else
escaped to solid, inland ground.
The only sounds
are the suck and spit of waves, the occasional
cackle and screech of gulls.

Not one car, truck,
or human voice.
Not even a distant rumble
of traffic. No dogs barking.
No slam of a screen door.

The absence of ordinary sounds
bears down, like the weight of water
    when we went diving, when weekends were a time
    not spent bagging ruined clothes and books,
    but pressure building the farther we sank,
    breathing the limited air strapped to our backs,
    hearing only our breathing through our regulators,
    blood murmuring in our ears.
No generators hum
as we wait for power to return.
The stars and moon still drown in clouds.

The air is black wool, black tar, black mud,
or sometimes, just before dawn,
the color of water,

>>like sometimes, when diving,
we can barely see our arms reaching out
of the surface, which churns and roils,
to grasp the anchor line
the compass tells us should be there.

One night the moon breaks through,
spreads stains of leached purple
across the last
vestiges of the storm's breath.

It's all we can do to breathe.

Our lungs swell
with the smells of retreating water and brine.
We, who elected to stay behind,
think we understand
what it means to be abandoned.
And then
the bridges and causeways open again.

The return and rebuilding,
the reconstructions of loss,
seem like more than I, you, or anyone can bear.

The Wrack Line

Dried fragments of paper birl
    around bits of brick, jagged boards, an occasional
        plastic trash can, puffs of fiberglass, small tablets of metal

blown off chimneys or other edges. Clumps of white sand,
    seaweed, and leaves streak the wide, black main street
        that winds through the neighborhoods,

the battered houses, closed shops and theater,
    then stops at a bridge or seawall.
        There are cars slouching along, again,

and the occasional truck, FedEx, UPS,
    electricians' and builders' vans, trash trucks.
        After the hurricane, white sand lay

piled like a blizzard across it all.
    Now the dunes have been piled high again
        on the beach, where they belong.

The kitchen and living room have dried out.
    The rugs, furniture, appliances are gone.
        He can't afford to replace them.

The mold, though, is contained, beaten back.
    The insurance will pay that contractor, at least. He returns
        the electric pump his neighbor loaned him,

which she will pass on to someone else whose basement
    is still flooded. He helps
        another neighbor rebuild his wooden porch.

Each hammer blow, each nail, each board
    helps them rebuild what they lost
        in the argument a year ago about where the neighbor's dog pees.

Later, someone else borrows a kerosene heater
    after discovering
        it will take several months to replace

the furnace the water drowned
    with the rest of her basement.
        The first time they met, he passed her,

sitting crouched on her front stoop, face in her palms,
    exhausted from hauling bags
        of water-logged clothes and books to the curb.

In the morning, he will meet more neighbors
    at a local deli, which is giving
        free coffee and doughnuts

to all living on this island.
    It will be enough to get them through that day.
        What he will remember most is the relief

the moment power came back, though
    it was only the kind that gives
        hot water, light, and heat.

There is never any other kind
    in places wracked by tides, wind, sand and waves,
        whose spindrift mists the air as the water curls and dives,

breaking against the bulkheads, dunes
    and boardwalk built to maintain a border
        that doesn't really exist and won't be contained.

The 21st Century Hurricane: An Assay

"There is something out in the dark that wants to correct us."

—Jane Hirshfield, "Against Certainty"

The ocean wants to correct
    our toxic habits by taking
        it all back: shells and rocks

ground down to a fine sand,
    coastal panic grass, bitter panicum, sea oats,
        gulls scavenging across the expanse of dunes,

thick layers of white sand
    piled like barrows across the small width of beach:
        the ocean wants it all back, again, again, again.

The waves wield foam and froth,
    slicing and stripping the coastline, bleeding sand across
        asphalt, concrete, driveways, garages, basements, kitchens, TVs

even bedrooms and hallways,
    clothes, rugs, blankets, books, and
        so much left to wallow in brine and mold.

Wind claws at brick and metal siding, jams
    its fingers into glass windows,
        snaps wooden rails and boards

while rain drowns concrete walls, slate roofs,
    wooden or plastic doors, asphalt roads, bridges,
        sand and wrack line. We think

there is only one eye to the storm:
    this is the calm of reconstruction.
        But the winds are circling again

around a faraway pole,
       bearing down,
            while our eyes focus

on the nails we hammer
       in decks and boards and floors we kneel upon.
           In the Arctic, a glacier melts:

the air above it flows toward us, disturbed in the ice's ecstatic freedom,
       like ondines riding the waves,
           bearing their deadly curse to surge through our sleep.

Saudade

At night she can only sleep in this tiny apartment
furnished with castoffs
if she pretends the sounds

of traffic along the freeway nearby
are the surf gently kneading the coastline
along this inland street. The rumbling

reshapes the parking lot into a stretch of beach
before a jetty and fishing pier. She used to see
the lights from casinos at the end of the island

and the spinning flashes of a Ferris wheel
from the next island, south of her anchor point.
Before the hurricane.

The sound of traffic has its own sporadic rhythm,
its own temptations for the dispossessed, the exiled—
it's hard for her to breathe here in PA.

She's used to the ocean's breath on her skin,
in her nostrils, the smell of brine and spindrift.
There is nothing here but trees and grass,

some hills in the distance covered by farms,
cornfields and cows, sparrows and crows,
the smell of manure and animals.

No gulls scratch the air with their hacking laugh,
only the deep cackle of crows. And more roads, black
with white and yellow lines she swerves in and out of

because she can, because there is nothing
to stop her, and she isn't even sure
of the speed limit on this stretch.

There is, she realizes one day, freedom in this
road, an emptiness that she can steer along
in her own way until another car passes, until another road

connects with this, and then there are houses, shops,
and people who don't care about wind and sand,
who only know streets and sidewalks and trees,

whose barriers are less obvious than bulkheads
but stronger and less open
to the abandon of tides.

IV.

A Snowy Winter

The neighborhood children imprinted
snow angels up and down the block,
ivory siding of the track homes
dull backdrops for the impressions

feathering across the layers of white,
pocked with foot and paw prints,
patches of black dirt and mud along the curbs
and driveways, plowed and shoveled mounds
eventually dumped over wings and feet. The angels

look around anyway. They watch
as children slip on ice and slide
to the school buses or waiting cars.
They rise into sentries, guards
of laboring furnaces, broken branches
dangling from limbs, cars crawling
on their bellies along icy streets.

Eventually sunlight melts the remainder
of their wingtips and halos.
Ice crystals
leak onto crocus bulbs, pushing green tips upward.
An angel perches on the top of a stamen,
another on the rim of a new bud,
a leaf, a bent stem.
They wait for the right moment.

They fly. The roofs
are black tar paper. The children
sleep quietly under thick down comforters.
Adults watch TV or type on computers.
Their flickering lights reflect in the glass windows.
The angels circle the neighborhood in one last flyby.

The children dream of drowning in cold, wet feathers.
In the morning, the air is tinged with warm light
and the absence of halos. Their flight path
has squeezed the sky into blues and greens.
The children's eyes sting
with a loss they cannot name. The adults
breathe lightly. They sing as they mow their lawns.

Moonshine

The angel enters a room, or tries. She can't
quite fit through the door. She folds
her wings tightly across her back
but the outer lines, curved like the frame
of a violin, still spread behind her,
frame her body, translucent with feathers
and cream instead of skin. She turns
sideways, sidles into the bar.
Two men have been watching.
Both have imagined her
in a different sexual position every seven seconds
since she opened the door.

It is evening, but the sun has not quite
sputtered out, and the angel dearly wants a taste
of the local moonshine though she doesn't
quite understand it's just whiskey.
The bartender, a woman, sees
only another woman undressed by the eyes
of the men watching her flow through the room.

Each man's fantasy centers on his own
preference for feathers or cream. One
wants to lick froth from her fingers and legs
as he watches her wings spread out toward the dying purple horizon.
The other wants to cling to her back, arms
wrapped around her neck, his body
poured between the thrusting pulse of her terrible,
white, plumed wings soaring them both into the haze of light dying
along the horizon. But the angel sits
at the bar, lifts a glass of moonshine
into the dim light of the room,
and stares in wonder
at the orange tint of malted rye.

Gristle

1.

The angel has no wings.
Its eyes, the color of wet concrete.
Its hair, shadows like black ivy
crawling along its back and shoulders.
Its fingers curl around a glass
it holds in the right hand, the left
spread flat across a table.
There is no one drinking wine
but the angel. There is nothing
but a piece of brown sky in the corner
of the window and small bubbles of sun
leaking across a wall, like tears
or dust motes, and the angel,
still holding a glass
shaped like an upside-down bell,
and silence. The angel listens
for the sound of feathers, gristle and wind,
but only a terrible heat glides along
the air currents and soot billowing across the city.

2.

The angel whirls, pirouettes, jetés
across a stage. There are mirrors.
Some people see a beautiful man.
Others, a woman.
His form is perfection, cocked and poised,
until she becomes a candle flame.
Then ash and charcoal.

3.

The air burns the lungs
of everything except angels.
Except the angels moved on
to where creatures listen
to feathers bristling with warnings.
Here, what is left:
gristle and bone,
concrete strangled by black ivy,
empty mirrors splintered
like wine glasses tossed out a window.

In an American City: Djinn Poem #1

The genie swirled like dust caught in an updraft,
    watching the museum's doors, people
        swerving before the wind, walking
around the column of distraught air.
    They couldn't see small streams of dirt
spill between his fingers like steady weeping.

They saw the museum's special exhibit,
    desert artifacts from Syria. The genie
        slipped through cracks in a window.
    The museum was gray stone walls,
glass cases, marble floors, alarms.
    The artifacts were silent: dull ivory knives,
broken scimitars, rugs the color of old blood stains and straw,
        tarnished brass bottles, cracked water jugs, a topaz ring,
glass beads, bows and arrows of wood dark like shadows.

    The genie mourned
with the bones. They whispered
    stories once told around fires
with roasting almonds and boiling tea.
    The bones hummed and prayed for sand,
        the abrasive desert night that cleanses.
    The genie's hands reached but could touch
only the passing wake of their voices,
    the memories of their prayers,
the sand, gravel, and clay they left behind,
    the ebb of their myths and families,
their decay and excavation.

The genie sang with them:
    a dirge for their exhumation.
        The walkers in the city outside felt

only an approaching storm, a dry rise
    in the air streams, dirt wafting
        from cracks in sidewalks and gates,
dust and exhaust, but no rain. Only a terrible
    wind that sang
        like tiny bells in the fringe of a veil,
the steady clinks of iron clasps of a saddle,
    the rising and falling voices
        of thousands of muezzins praying
        across immovable rooftops.

A Dragon that Can't Fly: Djinn Poem #2

The genie is loose in the city.
    He walks through Midtown, wondering
        how these humans speak
to objects rather than each other,
    how they close off what they can see
        with metal and concrete. He wonders
at buildings: who made such glass, and why
    such odd lines, such height? He smiles
        at a gargoyle carved into a stone lintel.
He hears a dragon screech and run beneath the street.
        He dissolves through a grate
in the black stench of a road. But the lights
    of the dragon's eyes strike so fast,
        he can only fade into the metal
bars that chain it. If he could free it,
    he thinks, he could ask about this place,
        he could know a creature
who can truly see him.
        Humans ride this tame dragon without gratitude.
He mourns its fire. He watches it lumber
    into a cave. Then he flies
        back into the stink and indifference
of air around buildings and streets
    to roam rooftops, passages above strange,
        metal creatures humans ride like horses,
like chariots, like camels across a desert of black tar.
    All around the sounds of storms
        blow through and back again below,
where the humans ignore
    the beams, walls and structures
    that herd people into paths
        they don't see clearly but use anyway,
bearing down on each other,
bearing down on the back of a dragon,
bearing down on the island as far as he can see.

Artifacts: Djinn Poem #3

The genie stands by a museum wall,
angels carved into the stone,
their wings folded together
like huge hands at prayer.
The stone, he thinks, must keep them
from flying. Beyond, a marble
sarcophagus, Egyptian mummies. Greek statues.
Lapis Lazuli collars, rings, sword hilts, and then,
finally, the artifacts of his people,
bones, and glass, like coffins with labels.

He can hear people move around him,
talking and pointing at the bones.
They do not understand
how centuries, an ocean, war, a desert
are not much space between them.
Such a small moment, and then he is sand
seeping through corners and hinges,
drifting around each knuckle, tooth, and rib
until he lies interspersed through them all,
rippling along memories and moments
when they were men and women.

All around, the museum lives
its usual kind of day. No one can hear
the gunfire, screams and bombs
in Syria, far away, not even the genie,
or the hand missing one tiny finger bone,
which is still trapped under a rock
just beyond what was once
the archaeologists' dig site,
where it had curled into the dirt and packed sand
that trucks and tanks now drive
over and over and over and over and over.

Feeding the Birds

Under a pink umbrella staked close enough
to the ocean to be cool, but far enough away
not to be engulfed by the rising tide,
a man sat on a yellow-striped beach chair
watching the warm surf, relaxing,
feeding a growing circle of seagulls
bread from his sandwich. He tried to eat
a few bites between tossing bits
to the fat, feathery predators
whose beaks snatched up the thick white bread,
demanded the meat slathered in mayo and oil, too.
They attacked his bag of fries
and the bag of chocolate chip cookies
but ignored the thermos of coffee by his feet.
He tried to eat quickly, to get as much as possible
for himself between tossing chunks outward,
but once he started feeding the birds,
he no longer possessed anything of his own.

The gulls moved in, pecking, greedy:
one flew up to his hands
and snatched what was left of the sandwich.
Another flew up to his face
and pecked at his eyes.
Another grabbed a finger in its beak and pulled,
as though stretching a clam muscle from its shell.
Another attacked his other hand's fingers,
and another flew at his mouth,
sliced his lips with its beak, eating chunks
of that flesh the way it might tear apart a starfish.
As he screamed, another scored its beak into his mouth
and ripped out his tongue, leaving him
gargling in his own blood and desires.

The gull flew away with its prize.
Others followed, screeching and trying to steal
the bloody muscle, which dripped, mute,
onto the sand, amid shrieks of possession and desire.
The thermos lay on its side, dripping coffee,
which merged with the man's blood
and bits of bone from his shredded fingers.
The caffeine gave one finger a few seconds of life.
It wiggled one end upward toward the sky.

Orectic

1.

Swallows skirr in formation
toward a distant copse of trees.
Somewhere, the scarecrow and tin man

are still winding their way through Oz
with no heart, no brain, no Dorothy, no witches,
only the magic they can make on their own.

Tornadoes are the summer's vengeance
on insurance companies:
local houses are sealed to the ground
tightly by concrete and asphalt.

Still, some little girls love to dance in red shoes,
will even glue on red glitter to make them sparkle
as they dance around the yard, pretending

to flee from flying monkeys, though, really,
those black wings are just crows hunting.

2.

The children's laughter and shouts
drift up and down the streets, invade
the open windows of the neighbors who think

of vanilla birthday cake with butter cream and coconut
icing with lemon filling, or chocolate brownies
sprinkled with walnuts, and mounds of pistachio ice cream.

Actually, the children are eating a simple
sheet cake from Costco with an icing drawing
of pirates waving from a ship spread over the yellow confection.

The birthday girl blows out the seven candles and wishes
her dad would stay there and not go home
to his other wife, and her mother wishes
she didn't have to see that same man again, ever,
and the father is sorry he came,
and the other children all want to break
the piñata and eat candy before anything else.

The mothers force dusty, hot smiles as they chat.
No one knows about the chemicals in the water
and ground these houses were so quickly built on,

though in ten years they will wish they had known, had never lived
in that small circle in the city built by a company bought up
in a hostile takeover about five years after that party.
Lawsuits will be futile. The Emerald City protects its emeralds.

3.

The body in the coffin looks like
a Muppet that has been thrown away.
Empty of the hands that gave it substance,
it lies flattened and colorless against the white pillow and lining.

The girl's mother can't breathe enough air,
her chest feels as though someone is trying to split her
breastbone with a hammer and large nail,
her stomach is full of mosquitoes and horse flies, biting, biting,
her mouth is cracked wood, like the railing of the deck
over the backyard behind her house.

The girl's classmates gather together to one side
of the funeral parlor room. Movies and TV shows
haven't prepared them for this. Their adolescent awkwardness
trumps the grief they don't quite know how to feel yet.

They will know its muddy flood
when she's not there to play a video game, or at band practice

when there is no clarinet playing slightly out of tempo to tease,
and no one to cheat off of in algebra anymore.

Now they just wonder why she looks like that,
what they should say to her mother. They are counting
on their own mothers to do that for them,
but their fathers nudge them over to the receiving line
and they have to hug her, they have to tell her
they will miss the girl, too. And they mean it.

They don't know she will be only a distant memory in a few years.
Two of them will join her, though buried in different cemeteries.
The others will move away. The houses will sell at a loss.
One father will declare bankruptcy, another, take a lower salary
two states away, and all will lose touch with everyone.

There is nothing, really,
they can say to each other, anyway.
The borders of Oz are impassable.

Blowing Bubbles

1.

Stink bugs keep sticking to the backdoor screen.
                                Please advise
My backyard sparks with lightning
bugs. The trees are on fire,
but the flames can't catch—
the bugs blink out too soon.
                                Please advise
The blackberry bush shrivels.
Below the fence are holes.
The cat buried the dead
jasmine flowers. The hot air
grows each day into brown fog,
burning my sinuses.
                                Please advise
I canceled the cable. The TV
could tell me nothing I already know.
The beta fish blows its bubbles because
that's what it knows.
Isn't it time to visit the dead?
                                Please advise

2.

Stink bugs have no known predators here in the US.
Have you learned to live with them?
Don't breathe when you crush them.
How many fireflies have you trapped?
Mason jars are best. Line them up on the railing.
Your porch will be rimmed by sparklers.
After the Fourth of July, let them go
if they are still alive. Close up your fence,

lock the gate, don't breathe. There will be
new bursts of pollen moving in the air.
If the dead have been digging in your garden,
it's time. It's just time.
All we know is still brown fog.

Who Speaks

1.

for the paper, lying
before the pen, writing
its own scrawled legacy in blue, black, red
or even green. The green ones, in particular,
have their own voice, scratched in a lined diction.
Who is there to say: hey, watch out,
those words cut to the nib, scar indelible ink here
on the finely ruled, stretched paper
laid blank before the pen's onslaught,
straight, hard, bearing
deep into the thick, absorbent layers
it teases with its swirling touch,
licking its finely inked tongue,
forever altering what the paper can bear
before it lies, eventually, vacant in a trash can.

2.

for the plastic water bottle,
drained of all but a thin stain
glistening at the bottom,
so many cracks and dents squeezed
into its ridged curves, its cap, shed
and lost to trash can or curb or
propped by the side of a gutter while the bottle
floats languidly along a sewer, trash barge,
or ocean current where gulls will peck at it;
or a dump, where it will lie in the sun,
unable to refract rainbows like glass,
where it will roll with gusts along a mound
of other bottles, paper, pens, and waste
of everything stagnant, rotting,

or unable to rot,
perpetually loose among the debris of lives
it has never touched, sliding through the refuse,
a little further down each year to the inner
middle of the pile, piled and piled.

3.

for the hands ungrasping
the pen, paper, bottle, trash bag
unfurling into the current airstream, riptide,
water flowing downriver and into whatever
waits at the end. The voices.
Who will speak for all of our hands
when we know, finally, we have
grasped too much?

Suicide Note

When I bought this house outside LA, three orange trees
blossomed in my backyard. The fruit was small and bitter.
I made jam from their orange pulp, processed sunlight. My front
lawn was made of stones and sand, but I grew antique roses
under the front windows: Climbing Iceberg, Winter Sunset,
Beaute Inconstante, Clytemnestra. Their scents
would swirl in variants of wind through open windows,
the screen door, into my nights and bed. I fed the yellowed, dead
petals scattered along the front of the house to my garden
with chips of wood, dirt, and water I sprayed
like rain over squash and tomatoes.

Today when I turn on the hose or open a tap on the sink only air
hisses out, and the pipes clank with the house's refusal to be
complicit anymore. My neighbor says
the government drained the reservoir and is storing our water
underground to sell to rich Arab countries. He's sure there is plenty
of water in the mountains we could pipe in here
if the government really wanted to. *You'll see,* he says, *you'll see
what they make us pay to get that water.*

I don't know why I let him talk to me.

The Internet says there is no more water in California. The roads
that run from here to Washington and Oregon are stalled
thick with cars and smoke from wildfires gorging on brush. It's dry
there, too, but the lines of autos at our northern border stretch and
stall. The TV said Arizona and Nevada dried up for good last week.
Maine and Vermont offered to take refugees.

I won't leave my orange trees. Their leaves are so brittle they have
curled inward like tiny, ancient scrolls. Not one fruit this year.
But I crave the bitter juice. With enough sugar and pectin,
the pulps became sun and water spread on toasted white bread.

Jars of jam are stacked in my basement still, waiting under layers
of sand and dust for me to taste their momentary relief.
Thirst spreads like seawater. Like conspiracies. The TV drones on
and on as I wait for someone to invent a way to find more water
and pipe it to us. The house waits, resolute but desolate,
like an ocotillo, branches splayed, brittle and dead
beneath unrelenting desert sun and wind.

The New Game Theory

Lake Mead is shrinking into a crater, Hoover Dam
into cracked concrete, dead turbines.
Paved and confused, NJ and NY
are refugees from the swelling Atlantic.
Nevada is buying out the entire country
because casinos own all the real estate,
that's all. We'll strike water eventually,
says the pundit on TV. The odds
are always in the house's favor.
Improvisation and all things Jersey
must surely trump mass extinction.
From Las Vegas to Atlantic City, the stakes
are all just a lot of damn theories.
We're all clamshells in the beaks of sea gulls.
Or at least mixed metaphors flopping around in a dry lake.

Acknowledgments

These poems have appeared in the following publications, to whose editors grateful acknowledgment is made:

Aji Magazine: "Artifacts: Djinn Poem #3" (as "Djinn Poem #3), "The End of Summer in Atlantic City"
Amarillo Bay: "How to Catch a Monarch," "Why They Sold the House"
American Literary Review: "Why the Wind Makes that Sound"
Apple Valley Review: "Nothing"
Apt: "Blowing Bubbles," "How to Deal with an Ex"
Broad!: "Nada"
Cog: "Driving Through Kansas"
Fledgling Rag: "Lancaster," "Preterition," "Saudade," "The 21st Century Hurricane: An Assay" (nominated for a 2014 Pushcart Prize), "This Oven Vault of a City," "Who Speaks," "The Wrack Line" (as "Birling")
Foliate Oak Literary Magazine: "Moonshine"
Jellyfish Whispers: "Driving Through Utah"
Kentucky Review: "Orectic," "Taps"
Peacock Journal: "Flight," "Ode to a Rug," "What the Tide Brings"
Rattle: "Surrender"
The Red River Review: "Talking to My Sister..."
Toasted Cheese: "Thanksgiving Dinner"
Voices: "A Dragon that Can't Fly: Djinn Poem #2"

"Driving Through Utah" appeared in *Storm Cycle 2014: The Best of Kind of a Hurricane Press* (Kind of a Hurricane Press, 2015).

"Malala," and "Malala's Mother: the First Week" appeared in *Malala: Poems for Malala Yousafzai* (FutureCycle Press, 2013).

"Through a Glass, Bitterly" was awarded 2nd place in the Yorkfest Adult Literary Competition, August 2015.

Special thanks to the Lancaster writers' group for all their support and advice, especially Seth Martin, who read the entire manuscript several times. Special thanks, also, to Madeleine Deininger for her support and encouragement. Thanks to Laure-Anne Bosselaar for her gentle but honest critique. And thank you to the Harrisburg Area Community College for giving me a sabbatical to complete this book.

Cover photo by the author; author photo by Lifetouch Portrait Studios Inc.; cover and interior book design by Diane Kistner; Adobe Garamond text with Cerigo titling

About FutureCycle Press

FutureCycle Press is dedicated to publishing lasting English-language poetry books, chapbooks, and anthologies in both print-on-demand and Kindle ebook formats. Founded in 2007 by long-time independent editor/publishers and partners Diane Kistner and Robert S. King, the press incorporated as a nonprofit in 2012. A number of our editors are distinguished poets and writers in their own right, and we have been actively involved in the small press movement going back to the early seventies.

The FutureCycle Poetry Book Prize and honorarium is awarded annually for the best full-length volume of poetry we publish in a calendar year. Introduced in 2013, our Good Works projects are anthologies devoted to issues of universal significance, with all proceeds donated to a related worthy cause. Our Selected Poems series highlights contemporary poets with a substantial body of work to their credit; with this series we strive to resurrect work that has had limited distribution and is now out of print.

We are dedicated to giving all of the authors we publish the care their work deserves, making our catalog of titles the most diverse and distinguished it can be, and paying forward any earnings to fund more great books.

We've learned a few things about independent publishing over the years. We've also evolved a unique, resilient publishing model that allows us to focus mainly on vetting and preserving for posterity poetry collections of exceptional quality without becoming overwhelmed with bookkeeping and mailing, fundraising activities, or taxing editorial and production "bubbles." To find out more about what we are doing, come see us at www.futurecycle.org.

The FutureCycle Poetry Book Prize

All full-length volumes of poetry published by FutureCycle Press in a given calendar year are considered for the annual FutureCycle Poetry Book Prize. This allows us to consider each submission on its own merits, outside of the context of a contest. Too, the judges see the finished book, which will have benefitted from the beautiful book design and strong editorial gloss we are famous for.

The book ranked the best in judging is announced as the prize-winner in the subsequent year. There is no fixed monetary award; instead, the winning poet receives an honorarium of 20% of the total net royalties from all poetry books and chapbooks the press sold online in the year the winning book was published. The winner is also accorded the honor of being on the panel of judges for the next year's competition; all judges receive copies of all contending books to keep for their personal library.

www.ingramcontent.com/pod-product-compliance
Lightning Source LLC
Chambersburg PA
CBHW070006100426
42741CB00012B/3127